# THE RICH AND THE POOR THINKING

What do the rich think about money - that the poor do not?

Robert A. Reyes

# Table of Contents

Chapter 1

The affluent create money

There's a tremendous gap between what the 1% invest in, and what the .001% invest in. For the uninitiated, the chasm between these two is measured in the of millions of dollars. But the value systems that drive the .001% are beyond anything financial or economic.

When you look at the ultra-wealthy, the .001%, what are they buying into? They're already financially well-established, so what are they purchasing at this point? Legitimacy. That's what they're purchasing. They invest in goods that increase their prestige, intellect, and social levels. This is shown in continued heritage and progression towards the highest echelon of society and riches. This is how they impose their rank and identity. It's a function of their brand; it's a reflection of who they are and how they want to be branded into eternity.

For businesses trying to impose individuality, boost personal prestige, and engage in this sandbox, here are three places where you should be exploring:

Sports team ownership

When you look at NFL club owners, they're wanting to network with others and find a means where money is not simply the lone barrier to entrance, it's reputational. If you're in, you're in. It's a network that is perhaps considerably more renowned than anything like it on earth. It crosses all sectors; you have venture capitalists, real estate developers, and everyone joining together to invest in these assets. It's a statement. It's beyond the nouveau riche

Ferrari. Behind your back, your friends and relatives claim they know the owner of an NFL or NBA club.

And this is universal. Professional sports leagues, European sports unions, and basketball, soccer, or other major league sports team in any big city.

When it comes to office buildings, it might be real estate in any nation.

"These structures represent the newest and finest quality buildings in their market. They are often the finest-looking structures with the greatest construction and boast high-quality building infrastructure. As a consequence of this, they attract the finest quality renters and charge the highest rates."

Making income from leasing and renting is secondary, it's already built-in and anticipated with corporate tenants who are household brands with significantly superior credit and balance sheets than most renters. But someone's going to leap from this asset to the tower because it provides them a chance to appear good in front of their peers, and on social media.

Fine art
Fine art is another, it's always been the credibility maker for many developing families. They invest in art and build a collection. They want to speak about the past, but actually, it's something that they possess that nobody else does. These are world-class statement assets that haven't lost value in decades, centuries in certain instances. To them, art is not only a good investment, but it's a highly respectable one. It's a statement asset.

Extremely expensive fine art has survived hundreds of years, it's always going to be there, it's solid world-class collateral if you know what you're doing and people play in those circles simply to claim that they're engaged in fine art.

Making an effect now and in the future the .001% prefer to invest in things that will make a difference. Making an impact involves investing in something amazing that benefits mankind but might also reward you with an outsized return on an investment that most will never experience in their lives. That's because the influence you're producing or linking your brand to is so prolific.

Space exploration, as well as remedies for viruses and illnesses, are what's next. These sorts of investments have been and will continue to be the ultimate sport of luxury. For decades, NASA, academic interests, and their restricted resources governed American space exploration and travel. Also, it benefits the government, since they provide private industry implicit clearance to commence their efforts because they are accepting the risks.

More individuals have more riches than ever before in the history of the globe. Think about it, there are 24-year-old Instagram influencers who have used media as a lever to make money quicker and easier than ever before in history. They're the ones who are going to continue to flourish, who will be the future leaders because they control their media.
People who own their own media today are the ones who are eventually going to control a large amount of wealth and influence capital flows. We're at the greatest moment of mankind right now, when there are simply so many riches

that individuals can do stupid things and prosper.

I never had access to money throughout my youth, or even as I developed into a teenager and young adult. Both of my parents lived paycheck-to-paycheck and battled with debt, so that's all I knew.

As a consequence, I was never truly exposed to the investment world, nor did I come to think of entrepreneurship as a feasible career choice. My parents were busy trying to keep the lights on and food on the table — the concept of having extra money to invest and generate wealth would have been strange to them.

Eventually, however, I received my first exposure to the fundamentals underlying investing and generating money. I studied finance in college, learned about mutual funds and ETFs, and found out how the stock market truly works.

The problem is, these are places where affluent people do spend time and time again. That's because they know something most others don't – they realize that increasing wealth is about more than pouring money into the stock market, becoming an entrepreneur, or taking enormous risks to support a great business.

Establishing money is just as much about being the greatest version of yourself, keeping in continual learning mode, and building a network of like-minded individuals who can help you attain your objectives.
Want to know precisely what I'm talking about? Here are some of the most typical non-financial investments affluent individuals prefer to make:

Accelerated Learning

Most affluent individuals read a lot of books published by people who inspire them in some manner or have a unique experience to offer.

Reading is such a clever and economical method to occupy part of your spare time and expand your knowledge, which is something the affluent already know. If reading a few hours each week might help you keep cognitively sharp as you learn new things, why wouldn't you make that option again and over?

But there are other techniques to increase learning that don't require reading or books. You may also take online courses on areas that pertain to your work.

Personal Coaching

"For those wishing to break through to the next level of achievement, I strongly suggest investing in coaching.

The thing that turns most people off regarding coaching is that it's not free; in fact, some coaching programs cost thousands of dollars. But affluent individuals realize the investment may be well worth it, which is why they're more than prepared to leap in.

Mentorship

Mentorship may also be crucial, especially when you are learning the ropes in your industry. One of the finest mentors I had was the first financial adviser who hired me. He was a million-dollar producer and had over a decade of experience under his belt. I quickly acquired access to his expertise as his office was only next door and, trust me, I learned as much as I could.

Mastermind Groups

It's usually reported that Dave Ramsey was in a genius group called the Young Eagles when he initially launched his firm. Entrepreneurs such as Aaron Walker and Dan Miller were also in the group, and they drew on one another for guidance and mentoring to acquire. I suppose most of the rich elite join in some form of mastermind group or club.

Mastermind groups are immensely beneficial because they allow you to bounce company ideas off other entrepreneurs who may believe differently than you but still have your best interests at heart. And sometimes, it's a simple bit of advice or a single phrase that may make all the difference in your business aspirations – and your life.

Building Relationships

When it comes to the upper ranks of the corporate world, there's one adage that's virtually always true: "It's not only what you know, but who you know.

"The appropriate contacts may help obtain better employment, hasten promotions, or create profitable businesses," he adds.

But it's not about corny networking events. To obtain the greatest value, concentrate on meeting individuals at professional conferences, mastermind groups, and high-quality membership communities.

This is a tactic most successful people know – meet other individuals that you admire and establish a friendship that is advantageous for everyone.

But, there's a catch – and this is key. When you meet someone new who might assist you in your company, you can't simply come out of the gate asking for favors. I strongly believe in the VBA technique — or "Value Before the Ask." This implies making sure you give value before seeking favor from anybody.

In other words, make sure you're doing your half of the effort to make the connection a win for everyone. If you attempt to create ties with other entrepreneurs simply so you can ride their coattails, you'll be kicked to the top.

Chapter 2

Knowing financial literacy

What Is Financial Literacy?

Financial literacy is the capacity to comprehend and successfully employ different financial abilities, including personal financial management, budgeting, and investing. The meaning of financial literacy is the cornerstone of your relationship with money, and it is a life path of learning. The sooner you start, the better off you will be since knowledge is the key to success when it comes to money.

The world financial literacy refers to a multitude of critical financial abilities and ideas.
Financially savvy people are often less prone to financial fraud.

A good foundation of financial literacy may assist support numerous life objectives, such as saving for college or retirement, handling debt wisely, and operating a company.

Key parts of financial literacy include learning how to construct a budget, prepare for retirement, manage debt, and monitor personal spending.

Financial literacy may be achieved via reading books, listening to podcasts, subscribing to financial material, or talking to a financial practitioner.

Understanding Financial Literacy

In recent decades financial goods and services have grown more ubiquitous across society.

Being financially illiterate may lead to a variety of dangers, such as being more likely to accrue unsustainable debt loads, either via bad spending choices or a lack of long-term planning. This, in turn, may lead to bad credit, bankruptcy, house foreclosure, and other undesirable repercussions.

Thankfully, there are now more resources than ever for anyone desiring to educate themselves about the world of banking. One such example is the government-sponsored Financial Literacy and Education Commission, which provides a variety of free learning tools.

Financial literacy may assist prevent people from being victims of financial fraud, a sort of crime that is growing increasingly widespread.

Scope of Financial Literacy
Although numerous abilities can come under the banner of financial literacy, prominent examples include household

budgeting, knowing how to manage and pay off loans, and analyzing the tradeoffs between various credit and investment options. These abilities frequently involve at least a rudimentary grasp of important financial principles, such as compound interest and the time value of money.

Other goods, such as mortgages, student loans, health insurance, and self-directed investment accounts, have also expanded in prominence. This has made it even more vital for folks to learn how to utilize them appropriately.

Financial literacy also involves short-term financial plans as well as a long-term financial strategy. Financial literacy comprises recognizing how investment choices made now may affect your tax bills in the future. This also entails learning which investment vehicles are ideal to employ while saving for retirement.

Benefits of Financial Literacy
Holistically, the purpose of financial literacy is to enable people to make wiser choices. More precisely, financial literacy is vital for a variety of reasons:
Financial knowledge may avoid disastrous blunders. Floating rate loans may have different interest rates each month, but standard IRA payments can't be withdrawn until retirement. Seemingly benign financial actions may have long-term effects that cost people money or disrupt life goals. Financial literacy helps people avoid making errors with their own money.
Financial literacy prepares individuals for crises.

Financial literacy themes such as saving or disaster planning help folks ready for the unpredictable. Though losing a job or having a significant unexpected bill are always financially damaging, a person may lessen the effect by practicing their financial literacy in advance by being ready for emergencies.

Financial knowledge may assist a person to attain their objectives. By better knowing how to budget and save money, people may build plans that set expectations, keep them responsive to their finances, and sets a route for accomplishing unreachable objectives. Though someone may not be able to finance a desire today, they can always establish a plan to better raise their chances of making it happen.

Financial knowledge induces confidence. Imagine making a life-changing choice without all the knowledge you need to make the best decision. By being equipped with the necessary information about money, people may approach big life decisions with better confidence recognizing they are less likely to be startled or adversely affected by unanticipated consequences.

Strategies to Improve Your Financial Literacy Skills

Developing financial literacy to enhance your finances entails studying and applying several skills related to budgeting, managing and paying off debts, and understanding credit and investment products.

Here are a few practical methods to consider.

Create a Budget—

Track how much money you get each month versus how much you spend in an Excel sheet, on paper, or using a budgeting app. Your budget should incorporate income (paychecks, investments, alimony), fixed costs (rent/mortgage payments, utilities, loan payments), discretionary spending (nonessentials such as dining out, shopping, and vacation), and savings.

Pay Yourself First—To build savings, this reverse budgeting technique includes establishing a savings goal (say, a down payment for a house), determining how much you want to contribute toward it each month, and putting that amount away before you divvy up the rest of your spending.

Pay Bills Promptly—

Stay on top of monthly invoices, making ensuring that payments routinely arrive on time. Consider taking advantage of automated debits from a bank account or bill-pay applications and sign up for payment reminders.

Get Your Credit Report—

Once a year, customers may get a free credit report from the three main credit bureaus—Experian, Equifax, and

TransUnion—through the federally established.

Review these records and dispute any mistakes by contacting the credit bureau of discrepancies. Because you can acquire three of them, try spreading out your requests over the year to check yourself often.

Having a strong credit score helps you acquire the greatest interest rates on loans and credit cards, among other perks. Monitor your score with a free credit monitoring service (or, if you can pay to and want to add a layer of safety for your information, select one of the top credit monitoring services) (or, if you can afford to and want to add an extra layer of protection for your information, use one of the best credit monitoring services). In addition, be aware of the financial actions that might enhance or reduce your score, such as credit inquiries and credit use ratios.

Manage Debt—

Use your budget to keep on top of debt by cutting expenditures and boosting payments. Develop a debt-reduction strategy, such as paying off the loan with the highest interest rate first. If your debt is considerable, contact lenders to renegotiate payments, combine debts, or locate a debt-counseling program.

Invest in Your Future—If your workplace provides a 401(k) retirement savings plan, be sure to join up and contribute the maximum to earn the corporate match. Consider starting an individual retirement account (IRA) and constructing a diverse investment portfolio comprising equities, fixed income, and commodities. If required, get financial guidance from expert advisers to help you evaluate how much

money you will need to retire comfortably and design methods to attain your objective.
Example of Financial Literacy

Joseph  is a high school teacher who seeks to tell her pupils about financial literacy via her curriculum. She instructs students on the foundations of several financial subjects, such as personal budgeting, debt management, education and retirement saving, insurance, investment, and even tax preparation. Joseph  thinks that while these disciplines may not be extremely relevant to her pupils during their high school years, they will still prove beneficial throughout the remainder of their life.

Understanding concepts such as interest rates, opportunity costs, debt management, compound interest, and budgeting, for example, could help her students manage the student loans that they might rely on to fund their college education and keep them from amassing dangerous levels of debt and endangering their credit scores. Similarly, she anticipates that some subjects, such as income taxation and retirement planning, will\seventually prove valuable to all students, no matter what they wind up doing after high school.

Why Is Financial Literacy Important?
The lack of financial literacy may lead to a variety of dangers, such as building unsustainable debt loads, either via bad spending choices or a lack of long-term preparedness. This, in turn, may lead to bad credit, bankruptcy, house foreclosure, or other undesirable repercussions.

How Do I Become Financially Literate?

Becoming financially literate entails studying and applying several skills related to budgeting, managing and paying off debts, and understanding credit and investment products. Basic actions to enhance your finances include setting a budget, keeping track of costs, being careful about regular payments, being smart about saving money, frequently checking your credit report, and investing for your future.

What Are Some Popular Personal Budget Rules?

Two regularly used personal budgeting approaches are the 50/20/30 and 70/20/10 guidelines, and their simplicity is what makes them popular. The former requires splitting your after-tax, take-home income pay into three areas—needs (50%), savings (20%), and desires (30%). The 70/20/10 guideline also follows a similar plan, proposing that your after-tax, take-home income be split into sectors that cater to costs (70%), savings or lowering debt (20%), and investments and charity giving (10%).

What Are the Principles of Financial Literacy?
There are five major concepts of financial literacy. Though alternative models may specify different important components, the overarching\sgoal of financial literacy is to educate people on how to earn, spend, save, borrow, and protect their money.

What Are Some Examples of Financial Literacy?
As high school student advances to college, they may be confronted with the difficult challenge of picking which school to attend and how to fund their education. This may involve how much

money they should be saving from their after-school employment, how the conditions of their loan will function, and what opportunity costs exist along their decision-making process.

In this scenario, the student will make more financially responsible judgments if they are more financially educated. Financial literacy in this scenario extends to savings, jobs, budgeting, loans, and financial planning. Using financial literacy and making wise choices, the student can set themselves up for long-term success.

Financial literacy is the understanding of how to make good choices with money. This involves setting a budget, knowing how much to save, determining advantageous loan conditions, comprehending the affects to credit, and identifying various vehicles utilized for retirement. These abilities help people make wiser judgments and behave more responsibly with their own money.

# Chapter 3

## Mind your own business

Entrepreneurs come in many forms and sizes. They may vary by age, gender, financial resources, employment histories, or skillsets. But all entrepreneurs have many common traits: they believe in the basic concept, are risk-takers, and are prepared to work hard. That may be the mix for a spectacular triumph. True entrepreneurs don't have a choice; they simply have to do it; they just have to try.

I've been an entrepreneur for years. I've created, operated, promoted, and sold firms and I've advised many more entrepreneurs along the road. Whether you're a brand new entrepreneur or one with years of experience, these recommendations should be of benefit.

Valuable Tips for Entrepreneurs

1. Coming up with a concept is the most fun; implementing it...not so much. The concept is around 1% of the whole company while execution is about 99%. In other words, the day-to-day job is where success rests.

2. Most individuals only think about how fantastic their concept is. They don't think about how they will let others know about their wonderful concept. Figure out how you're going to advertise your company, and to whom (Who's your audience?), before you invest too much time or money in your concept.

3. Take criticism. Talk to them about your concept, and show them what it does or how it works. Listen to what they

have to say. You will not like everything you hear or embrace all of the proposed adjustments, additions, deletions, or criticisms, but it's all useful.

4. Being an entrepreneur is not a get-rich-quick-scheme. Most companies are not instant successes. The greatest approach to succeed, and earn money, is to work for the company, daily, for a long time. Even if your firm is feasible, you may not break even for three or four years. It may take much longer to demonstrate a profit.

5. You will be most successful managing a company that you enjoy (or love!). Determine where your interests lay and what your passions are. Figure up a company that incorporates some or all of them. Making a lot of money should not be one of those things. Do something you

can't wait to do, and the money will come.

6. Always have a contingency plan. What if things go wrong...or right? Do you have the financial, strategic, operational, or marketing strategies in place to address what happens if you have too little, or too much, business?

7. Strive to be as enthusiastic about your company after 20 years as you were when you began. Continue to study your market, create new objectives, extend your brand, and most of all, push yourself to grow, evolve and enhance your company.

8. Do what you know. Use the information, experience, and skills you've obtained to start your firm. Do what you know... but do it differently, more efficiently, more cost-effectively, more

sustainably, or in a manner that will increase outcomes. Reinvent a better wheel.

9. Brand from the beginning. Take the time (from the outset) to establish a Mission Statement, a Vision Statement, a Positioning Statement, and a Core Values Statement. If you lose your path, they may set you back on the correct course.

10. Offer something no one else does. Become the unquestioned heavyweight in your field or build the widget with "wow!".

11. Work like you're being paid. Get up every day and put the hours in – whether someone's paying you or not. Make the time... back burner jobs don't succeed.

12. Set objectives for yourself and your company. Write them down. Be responsible to someone or yourself.

13. Work backward: determine where you want to go and then work out the steps to get there.

14. We all have a favorite job; something we'd rather be doing. Don't address only your favorite area of your company but be cognizant of the operational, financial, marketing, and strategic strategies that need to be in place to make your firm a success.

15. Be realistic as to the number of companies you wish to develop. A firm you manage by yourself may sustain your lifestyle as well as a business that employs a dozen people (and with a lot less stress) (and with a lot less stress). If feasible, develop a scalable firm.

16. Do it for the right reasons – not because you want to impress. Do whatever you do effectively and you'll win both personal happiness and the regard of others.

17. Don't quit. When you reach a wall and think, "I simply can't do this anymore," keep going. My training as an endurance athlete taught me that when you question you can continue, when your brain yells, "Stop!" is when you have to swim 10 more strokes, run 50 more steps or merely ride to the top of the hill. By the time you've gone just a little farther, the situation has usually shifted and you'll discover can keep going.

A small company is the fastest growing sector in the United States and accounts for 54% of all sales in the US (Source: SBA) (Source: SBA). There are various reasons why the industry is developing so quickly.

But if you're an entrepreneur, or would want to start your firm, you already know why. And if you have not begun is time to start. While you should research, evaluate, and surround yourself with inspiration, the route to being a rich entrepreneur begins with your head. Your mentality is the cornerstone for producing money. Without the appropriate money perspective, you'll never see the route to generating wealth. It's why so many lottery winners go bankrupt or the tales we witness of big-name entrepreneurs whose firm is now a house of cards due to their money practices.

Becoming a successful entrepreneur begins with a goal and a route of building a wealth mentality and connection with money. Here are four mentality adjustments that help entrepreneurs walk the route to prosperity and success.

1. Root out all kinds of scarcity

Have you looked at anything you wanted to purchase – something you needed — and thought, "that's expensive"? It might be a pair of running shoes or a new MacBook. If you thought about it rationally, the value is there, but you let a scarcity mentality persuade you that the first thing you should worry about is the price.

Have you ever considered hiring a coach, consultant, or taking a course, but you balked at the five-figure price? Assuming the service or service provider could provide – how much extra value would flow to your business?

A scarcity attitude is the basis of all money troubles. It's what hinders entrepreneurs from achieving that next level of development. It also shows itself in other ways, such as coming off anxious to get the sale with a prospective customer.

Scarcity repeals wealth and the potential to create income. Realize that there are 4.5 billion users of the Internet every day. In 2019, e-commerce sales exceeded 3.5 trillion dollars, according to Statista.

There is more than enough opportunity and money for those prepared to strive to achieve it. Change your perspective towards money as the first step to creating it.

2. Refuse to take less than the value you give

You're an entrepreneur. You've established a company that offers value. You may and should charge a reasonable amount for what you supply.

When circumstances are tight and sales are sluggish, there's a tendency to make offers to complete transactions. The problem is that you're destroying your positioning with your market, and you're instructing your customers only to purchase your goods and services at discount.

Don't compromise your pricing. When was the last time you saw a Rolex on sale? Your goods and services are Rolex levels – stop letting people obtain your Rolexes at Walmart costs.

Wealth creation comes when you're deliberate about asking a reasonable price and refuse to take less than you deserve.

3. Let the door strike them on the way out

As you refuse to compromise on your rates and root out scarcity, you'll have customers who will test your determination. They'll attempt to barter, pay late, complain when there's no cause to, and obtain more than they paid for.

You've heard it before, but you can't be scared to let customers go or outright fire them. Let that door strike them as they go onto a new service provider as you restore sanity.

Wealthy entrepreneurs concentrate on working with ideal clientele. They take on and retain those who are a good fit. Not every customer is appropriate for your company. The route to prosperity is packed with customers who make business pleasurable and what you envisioned.

## 4. Step into your revenue-earning potential

We spoke about the prospects online. There has never been a period in history where so many customers are all in the same spot. If you're going to become a prosperous entrepreneur, you have to release your inner Phoenix and step into your ability to earn.

You have to start each day focused on your company and activities that create cash. When you engage with customers, it may be tempting to become buried in client satisfaction – you have to put your company first.

Optimize how you spend your time, don't be hesitant about marketing and selling what you provide, and accept more sales discussions (after screening) (after vetting). Know your figures and establish what seems like unachievable objectives. You can accomplish this.

It's a terrific moment to become a rich entrepreneur and tap into the potential all around us. Change your money perspective and go on the road to building wealth, independence, and the flexibility to spend your time doing what works for you.

Chapter 4

Overcoming hurdle

Some individuals regard difficulties as a puzzle to solve. Some view setbacks as a chance to progress. Others regard impediments as dangers. Still, others interpret hurdles as implying they cannot achieve. Your perspective of hurdles to reaching your objectives impacts how you behave.

If you regard barriers as the world being against you or as implying you failed, then you are likely to be overwhelmed with unpleasant thoughts and uncomfortable emotions when confronted with blockages to your ambitions.
Perhaps you don't feel thoughts when presented with an issue. Maybe you instantly sense dread or humiliation.

Fear advises you to leave the situation, that you are in danger. Shame drives you to hide. If the circumstance isn't one in which you need to be terrified or humiliated, these feelings come in the way of your conquering problems. (Other emotions that you could feel also encourage you to perform particular behaviors that might or might not be useful. To learn more about your emotions and the activities related to the emotions, check this amazing atlas of emotions.)

Either your thoughts or your emotions or both might drive you to stop working on your objectives. You lose your passion. Perhaps you get resigned and no longer think about your objectives or what's essential to you. Your responses to difficulties kept you from attempting.

Think about the last hurdle you encountered. What thoughts did you have? What feelings did you have?

Were your responses to the last hurdle you confronted accurate? Were they helpful? What is your tendency of reacting to obstacles?

Discouragement, wrath, and grief are among the feelings that you could experience when presented with a barrier. These feelings might prevent you from striving to tackle the hurdle.

Maybe you blame yourself or others because your route to your objective is hindered. Those ideas might convince you to quit pursuing your objective.

The fact is that accomplishing most objectives entails overcoming hurdles. That's natural and part of the process. There's a remark by Frank Clark, "If you discover a route with no barriers, it usually doesn't go anywhere."

Sometimes difficulties can be overcome, and sometimes they can't. Sometimes you have to work around them or discover alternatives. The trick is to not quit up without sensible thinking because you hit a hurdle or because of your emotional response to the impediment.

Skills for the Wise Consideration of Obstacles

1. STOP. This is an ideal opportunity to employ the STOP skill from Dialectical Behavior Therapy. STOP stands for Stop, Take a step back, Observe, and Proceed carefully.

Take a step back and study your feelings. Let your emotions relax. Then view the obstacle as you would if it were someone else encountering it. What would you advise someone else to do?

2. Practice radical acceptance. Whatever objective you desire to attain will require overcoming difficulties. Expect hurdles and embrace them as part of accomplishing the objective. Of course, you don't want that. No one does. And most frequently the fact is there will be hurdles.

3. Accept your feelings. When you confront a hurdle, you'll feel emotions. Of course, you will! That's normal. Take a pause and spend some time relaxing. The aim is to not allow your emotions to stop you from doing what you can. Get into a "wise mind," which can think rationally to examine the emotional costs of pursuing a goal (Is it worth it?) and the realities of the situation.

4. Use your "intelligent intellect." Make choices regarding barriers with your intelligent mind: Your emotional mind will push you to stop, behave impulsively, anger, or give up when presented with impediments to your objective. Wait for your smart intellect to be in command. Your clever mind can take in new knowledge, be flexible in examining options, and be creative in thinking of answers.

5. Be open to investigating new strategies to attain your objective. In Radically Open DBT, Lynch alludes to being in a "flexible mind." A flexible mind is open to fresh ideas and new solutions. Knowing what doesn't work to bring you to your objective helps you to conceive of alternatives that could work. Learning that the route you initially picked doesn't work is disheartening, but at least you

know what doesn't work. That's critical information.

Maybe you wanted to be a teacher, but you can't find the money to go to school. What would be an alternative? Think about what it is about teaching that you enjoy. If you enjoy assisting children, then think of different methods to accomplish that. Maybe becoming an assistant teacher or working with youngsters at a daycare. Maybe you could teach a talent that you have, such as playing the piano or swimming.

Use your imagination. What else may be an alternative?
You might also work on strategies to get the money to go to school. You may consider taking even one class at a time.

6. Find meaning. When we endure challenging conditions, it's

uncomfortable, to say the least. At the same time, you may frequently discover significance in the hurdles you experience. Ask yourself: What lesson can I gain from this? Does this contribute to my life or my knowledge in any way?

I'm a cancer survivor. From having cancer, I learned that when you first hear of anything terrible or unwelcome in your life is the worst period, possibly second only to uncertainty. When you initially hear about a barrier, it may feel more intimidating than it will after you have thought about it.

Once you realize and accept that an issue exists, then you may work on addressing the problem or on drastically accepting the condition. The overpowering sensations go down. Lack of acceptance hinders you from working on the solution or from accepting what you can't alter.

Look for what you can learn from the challenges you face or have experienced.

7. Be willing to ask for feedback. Asking for ideas from others is an interpersonal skill. Getting knowledge from other individuals may be extremely beneficial in conquering challenges. Other individuals are likely to know resources that you don't, and they will have ideas that you may not have thought about. They also perceive the world differently than you do and may see answers you don't. Ask more than one individual.

8. Set minor objectives that lead to the main aim. Obstacles may be complicated and demanding. Achieving objectives might be tough and daunting with everything that you need to accomplish. It's hard to maintain motivation strong over time. Break down what you need to do to overcome the issue into

manageable stages. Focus on one step at a time. For example, if you want to learn to create more friends, then minor objectives may start with spending more time with others.

9. Mistakes are natural. As definitely while the sun rises every morning, you'll make errors as you strive toward your objective. It's simply part of being human. If you find yourself criticizing others or yourself, or blaming others or yourself, simply notice those thoughts and let them go. Remember nonjudgmental thinking. Acknowledge the error is there, and look at what you need to do next. Blaming discourages you, wastes your energy, and doesn't help fix the situation. Don't allow making errors to stop you.

10. Reevaluate. Sometimes what you think you desire turns out to not be right

for you. It's common to work toward a goal and then adjust your goals along the road. Part of working toward a goal is acquiring more knowledge and knowing more about what you are working for.

You could decide you want to run five days a week. As you strive toward the objective, you find that you prefer to pursue alternative things and that you are bored with jogging every day. You adjust your objective to doing something physically active or to taking dance classes instead.

11. Celebrate! Recognizing your successes is so very crucial. Celebrate the modest steps you take. This enables you to remain motivated and to recognize that you can achieve anything. It helps you concentrate on what you do achieve, not merely on the challenges or what doesn't work out.

If an impediment can't be overcome, and you can't find an alternative to your objective, then rejoice that you put the effort in and tried your best. Use your flexible, intelligent intellect and conceive of another aim that you wish to pursue.

Think about these steps. Which ones do you do effectively, and which ones might you add to your technique of conquering obstacles?

Obstacles are the stumbling obstacles that impede you from accomplishing your objectives. They are the restricting elements that impede you from accomplishing your desired ambitions, and you have to conquer these barriers to progress forward in life.

It's not enough to create objectives; you need to realize your ambitions. It is at the moment of execution that life gets terrible when unanticipated setbacks and difficulties kick in.

It is not an understatement to say that every accomplishment comes with hurdles. Those difficulties typically arrive as issues you need to address. If you can solve them, you may then have the certainty that you can attain your objectives.

Reasons Why Obstacles Are Important
So why is it vital to overcome obstacles? Can you travel through life without facing any limitations?

1. Obstacles Reveal You're True Identity
Some life crises will break you apart. When this happens, you get to know who you are. Sometimes, you don't know your complete talents and inclinations.

Obstacles exist to test you and strain you beyond bounds.

The reality is after your limits and tendencies have been disclosed, you can begin to take actions to cope with them so you may win in life. You'll be pushed to conquer these hurdles, which will help unveil your genuine nature.

2. Obstacles Direct Your Actions
Someone once told me you could walk on water; you simply need to know where the stones are put. The stumbling hurdles on your route generate a fresh approach to advance to the next level or phase.

For instance, if someone constantly damages your emotions, the scenario enables you to practice the art of forgiving. Every difficulty comes with its remedy. You simply need to alter your viewpoint to unearth the lessons that adversity has to offer you.


3. Obstacles Make You Tougher
No one comes with the innate capacity to resist hardships; you have to build your resilience through life. And don't you ever imagine everything will come to you on a platter of gold. That only occurs in the grave

As long as you are here, you'd have to conquer hurdles and surmount challenges. The point of hurdles is to toughen you so you can be fearless. It would be ideal if you ventured to alter your circumstances - to better yourself and the world.

And if you notice you are losing bravery, challenges might toughen you further so you can advance to the next step.

Make Every Minute of Your Life Count!

## 4. Obstacles Enable You to Focus on What Counts

Not everything matters in life, therefore you need to concentrate on your objectives and follow your life missions. Once you are clear about your objectives and duties, any hurdle that comes your way appears smaller and achievable.

But when you lack signals and direction, this uncertainty increases every barrier and makes your goal a gigantic mountain that you need to scale.

The main lesson is that you need to be clear about your objectives and concentrate like a laser so\syou can climb the few mountains that demand your attention.

5. Obstacles Unleash Your Creativity
You don't know how far you can run until you encounter a lion in the wild. That's the beauty of life!

Without barriers, you may not approach the untrodden terrain. It requires continuing and refusing to learn when others fail because they were impatient. Obstacles are capable of straining your creative muscles so you may push beyond the limitations.

6. Obstacles Help You Find Meaning in Your Life
Your view of life impacts your outcome. You may wish to draw a hint from the experience of President Abraham Lincoln. While he suffered with melancholy all along, he led the United States through one of the most arduous moments in history: The Civil War.

He discovered purpose and found succor in a more prominent cause higher than his hurdles.

7. Obstacles Can Help You Discover Meaning Beyond Your Inner Troubles
Just like Lincoln, you may discover your purpose when you halt looking at your worries and begin to explore how you might make others happy. You may climb beyond your barriers by boosting others.

This tactic is one of the greatest ways to cope with depression. It is a means of depriving your difficulties of time so you may concentrate on others suffering.
Ways to Overcome Obstacles in Life

1. Find Out What's Limiting You
Sit down and examine your limiting circumstances. What are the hurdles standing between you and your goals?

Figure out why you are not reaching the deadline. Avoid digging up your list of grievances since it will ultimately turn into excuses.

For instance, if you said,' I don't have adequate time,' concentrate on what you spend your time and energy on. Your limiting factors might be procrastination, complacency, or external circumstances. If you stated, 'I don't have enough funds,' this is most times connected to priorities.

Your immediate obstacle may be a lack of ambition or time, or you need to commit to learning how to create more revenue and minimize your spending.

2. Review the Obstacle's Timeline
How long have you been coping with the challenge? What attitude or habit is keeping you from conquering the obstacles? Finding answers to these

questions will help you to make the correct modifications.

For instance, if you changed your career, there might be something about your new job or workplace that is challenging you. It might be the fact that you need to adjust to new surroundings.

Reflect on the numerous hurdles you have experienced in life. Whether you work over them or not, take a hint from your experience and use the lessons in coping with fresh issues.

3. Determine What's Beyond You
Some difficulties are beyond you. They are so daunting that you don't have a clue on how to overcome them. Perhaps, you are even terrified or weak to the bone.

It shouldn't be the end of the world. Just take a deep breath and identify those things you can manage, such as:

Your habits
How much energy do you exert
Your choice when you have presented a chance
Your lifestyle-exercise, nutrition, and relaxation, all of which impact your mood and personal disposition
Focus on what you can control. Start with building all the positive habits to have in life.

4. Break Your Goals Down
A giant stride is not about taking one jump to the summit of the greatest mountain; it is about daring to follow your objectives in the face of opposition. It's appropriate to separate your objectives into parts and build a checklist

to find out the barriers blocking you from actualizing the first box.

For instance, if you aim to be the finest copywriter in the world, one imminent challenge is to enroll and follow through with an online course. Thus, your new aim may be to apply for an online class on copywriting. You may surpass this difficulty by opening your Google browser right now.

5. Maintain an Active Plan
Always work with a to-do list. Begin your day with what you have to accomplish and reach your objective. Recognize that there will be hurdles and diversions. The lessons from facing obstacles will help you to adapt your plan in finding the best strategy for achieving your goals.

6. Improve Your Problem-Solving Skills

If you prefer to make judgments based on your intuition, you may strive to be more analytic.

Here are some ways you may apply to make a decision:
Worst case scenario: If I join the copywriting course and I fail, where would I wind up? Design a backup strategy for this situation.

Cost-benefit analysis: What would I gain if I finish the copywriting course? Assess whether the advantages are worth the costs.

7. Track Your Progress
As you pursue your objectives, maintain a diary of your triumphs and problems. Establish milestones and pay yourself when you accomplish each milestone. There are four actions you may take to monitor your progress.

Final Thoughts

Obstacles give life significance. As long as you remain on the face of the world, you will keep confronting problems. It's up to you to modify your perceptions and cope with problems with the proper mentality. It's either they become your stepping stones or stumbling barriers.

Chapter 5

Building your wealth with a brand

"I want to establish a modest company and hope to become rich. Do I need to start a specific sort of business? Do I have to give up my personal life? What does it take to become rich?"
Rich individuals come from different sorts of industries. It's feasible to make wealthy in a limitless number of enterprises.

What's more, you do not need to be brilliant. You do not have to be a workaholic. You do not need to have any particular ability if you want to grow wealthy, either.
Another prevalent myth is that you must be in a high-flying business. There are lots of affluent company owners in typical daily firms (but you must select a

lucrative business - more below) (although you must choose a profitable business – more below).

Here's the secret most folks don't know. The most popular strategy to grow wealth is to be disciplined, make smart money choices and manage your funds wisely.

That's it.
Getting wealthy is about how you live your life and operate your company, and what you do with the money you earn.
So, returning to your question: how can individuals make wealthy in a tiny business? Mostly through adopting positive attitudes and money habits in their enterprises and personal life. They have financial discipline. They handle their money properly. And that's something everyone can learn to do.

To become wealthy perform these steps:

1. Start your Day Early

Early birds that start work early before others swear by the productivity and creative boost. Each day you have a handful of undisturbed hours before customers and workers start contacting you. You also profit from more thinking and planning time.

The more time for concentration, the more you can concentrate on how to think of fresh prospects to earn money from. It's not about working harder, simply smarter. Give yourself undisturbed time to ponder, make objectives, and plan.

If you are a determined night owl, you may be able to obtain the same advantage — but after hours. It's the same thing, except in reverse. You are working while others are not. This will help you create riches.

## 2. Have the Courage to Take Risks

As a collective, entrepreneurs and company owners tend to have a greater tolerance for accepting risks than the general population.

"You've come up with a concept, and your gut and instincts tell you it's a fantastic idea, be prepared to take the risk. But evaluate the choices you make and be prepared to confess when you made a terrible one and alter it and rectify it," he is reported as adding. He sold the firm and ultimately it became a billion-dollar enterprise.

Nothing risked, nothing gained. Be prepared to take chances if you want to grow wealthy. But, enter into it with eyes open and safeguard the downside by handling the risks wisely.

3. Live Below your Means

If you want to grow wealthy and remain affluent you have to save and not let your money flow out the door. Many prosperous individuals live below their means. Whatever their income is, they spend less than they make.

Wealthy individuals appreciate a deal like the rest of us. For example, one survey by Reuters indicated that millennials love shopping at dollar shops. About 29% of millennials who shopped there earned over $100,000 each year.

If you can gather money early, you can invest it and make it grow. Rich business owners:

Do not dwell in the largest home in the neighborhood.

Do not dine out at costly restaurants every night - they keep it for special occasions.

Avoid the trappings of a costly lifestyle (clothing, trips, etc) (clothes, travel, etc.) Their neighbors may appear affluent but remember they may not fact be rich since they spend everything they make. Rich people, by contrast, recognize that spending like you are rich is not the way to become rich. They got wealthy first. Later when their income is bigger they spend.

4. Stick with It; Wealth Accumulates
Slow and steady wins the riches race. Set objectives to collect riches and get prosperous, year after year.
A surprise windfall is great. Who wouldn't want to win the lottery or acquire an inheritance? But that's not how most people get wealthy.

Adopt the appropriate money practices, and the passage of time is one aspect that helps you grow wealthy. According to one survey by Ramsey Solutions, the majority of affluent individuals required 28 years to attain a 7-figure net worth. Nearly three-fourths of millionaires were aged 55 or older.

Time itself helps you grow affluent.

Young entrepreneurs in your 20s and 30s, take heart. You may be collecting money and on your road to becoming wealthy even if you haven't attained that magic 7-figure number yet. Year after year, whatever money you gain will increase provided you invest it. These days it's not hard to invest in mutual funds. You can do it online,
grow prosperous through time.

5. Pick a Business with Profit Potential
Rich folks select a firm with cheap operational expenses and strong profit

potential. Thousands of different enterprises and sectors suit this criterion. Avoid firms with significant operational expenses unless you are capable of acquiring outside financing. An example of a firm that would take several years to become successful would be a biomedical startup – because of the long development and regulatory approval procedure.

Most of us desire something that kicks off earnings far quicker. Also, to make wealthy without running yourself ragged, select a basic company. For suggestions of the sorts of enterprises that might help you get wealthy, read Most Profitable Small Businesses.

## 6. Run a Tight Ship

In a small firm, poor running procedures cost money in unseen ways. Sloppiness drains profits. Rich small company entrepreneurs run a tight ship.

Be hands-on. Inspect the minor things. Broken equipment, casual scheduling, messy premises — these lend to a general aura of carelessness that rapidly spreads like it is infectious. The flip side is, that paying attention to details may convert your firm into a lean, mean, profit-generating machine. Details make the difference between:

Happy repeat customers (or not!).

Products and services have such a fantastic reputation that they are simple to sell (vs ones with bad web ratings) (versus ones with horrible online reviews).

Equipment and vehicles that operate reliably (instead of frequently breaking down causing missed deadlines or excessive expenditures) (instead of constantly breaking down causing missed schedules or extra costs).

Expect everyone in the firm to pay attention to details. Create a "tight ship" culture. Lead by example and demonstrate why details are crucial. Encourage workers to take pleasure in working in a well-run firm. It will pay off for you and also coaches them in what it takes to manage a firm to become affluent.

## 7. Become a Frugal Business Owner

Rich company entrepreneurs are noted for being frugal about corporate expenditure, not just personal spending. Create a company budget and stick to it. According to one survey, a remarkable 93% of affluent individuals claim they generally stick to the budgets they make. There's a useful test to take before taking on any additional business cost. Ask yourself, "how many sales do I have to earn or how many hours of staff time do I have to pay for, to cover this expense?"

When you put it that way, a suggested expense may not be needed.

Switch from monthly payments to yearly if you are positive you will utilize the service or product. Many companies offer 10% to 20% savings for a yearly commitment.

These changes may seem modest, but it's simpler to grow wealthy when frugality becomes a regular habit. Also, it needs to be more than YOU being a tightwad. Make frugality part of your organizational culture. Rich company owners educate staff, particularly managers, to examine every cost.

8. Pay People Well

The best practice is to pay your employees the maximum you can afford, by industry pay standards. This may appear to contradict the instruction to be frugal, yet it is consistent.

Paying people properly decreases hidden expenditures like staff turnover, customer-souring bad attitudes, and low productivity owing to poor morale. In the long term, it's less costly to pay for competent support and decrease turnover.

You may get away with paying an extremely modest salary for a time. But when the job market is growing it finally catches up and you lose your finest talent. Treat workers as an asset. They may assist increase the business riches and their wealth at the same time as building yours. It's a triple victory.

9. Collect Receivables Timely
Believe it or not, one of the reasons the small company
owners do not grow wealthy because they do not collect their money.

Imagine you and your team labor your fingers to the bone, metaphorically speaking. Yet all the hard effort doesn't pay off. You are tremendously busy, yet end up unprofitable. 'How could this happen?' you ponder. The two offenders are:

Failure to Collect

You may be amazed at how many company owners just neglect to deliver invoices to customers. They don't have a system and are disorderly. So the owner ends up working for nothing.

Slow Paying Customers

Routinely waiting for 60, 90, or even 120 days to be paid wreaks havoc with the financial flow, producing a domino effect. The firm might be obliged to take up costly merchant advances, or hit expensive credit cards merely to pay the rent. You wind yourself paying additional loan costs.

A major performance measure that a wealthy small company owner watches is Days Sales Outstanding (DSO) (DSO). This gauges the length of time it takes to collect bills. In a well-run corporation, the DSO average is under 30 days. A DSO reaching 60 days or longer suggests weaker performance, however normal collection timeframes vary by industry.

10. Understand Taxes and Investing
Rich small company entrepreneurs recognize that savvy tax tactics and finance solutions produce wealth. If you want your money to grow, put it to work for you.

Also, understand how to take advantage of tax reduction options - lawfully of course. Take advantage of the top tax deductions for small companies.

Many affluent individuals think that tax-deferred assets like Individual Retirement Accounts or 401(K) plans are crucial to growing rich. For company owners, you have even more alternatives like Simplified Employee Pension (SEP) and Savings Incentive Match Plan for Employees (SIMPLE) plans.

Learn the benefits of compound annual growth rates. The potential of compound yearly growth may convert a small 401(K) into something much bigger over time. Adding consistent deposits to your investments, such as 10% of your salary, also has significant potential to generate wealth. That is what it means to make your money work for you to grow wealthy.

Whatever money you make, follow the example of wealthy company entrepreneurs. They treat with respect the money they make. They recognize that the key to getting wealthy is to build habits that provide them the opportunity to acquire assets and earn more money, year after year.

I believe that being wealthy in a company will still eventually rely on how effectively you save money. Overspending will still leave you bankrupt no matter how much you are earning.

The DSO (Days Sales Outstanding) is one indicator of business success however having a 30 or fewer day DSO doesn't always suggest that the firm is properly managed. Nor does a 60-day DSO suggest that a firm is not properly managed or will not survive. I have been in the company for 38 years and conduct unique services for extremely big corporations. They have master agreements that set payment durations of

60 to 90 days. Am I delighted with that? Not exactly, however, on the 60th day following the invoice date I know, I will get the cash for payment of an invoice. I can forecast cash flow very precisely. Of course, I have other smaller firms that do pay around the 30-day mark for the same sort of labor. You may claim that I don't have to sign the master agreement with a 60-day payment on bills. That is accurate, however, if I don't then I will not be able to undertake work for the firm. In other words, the master agreement is non-negotiable. Some organizations accept early payments however they maintain a portion of the invoice for enabling an early payment of an invoice to be made.

I have been a victim of spending in any way and have no budget for the company which leads to business failures, I will stop it.